THE QUESTKIDS™
DO CODING

Create Your First Website

in easy steps
CHILDREN'S BOOKS

You will need:

- A computer or laptop
- Text editor (Notepad, TextEdit, Sublime Text)
- Web browser (e.g. Chrome, Microsoft Edge/Internet Explorer, Firefox, Safari)
- Internet connection (for your web browser)

What is HTML?

HTML stands for Hyper Text Markup Language. It's the standard language that allows you to create websites for anyone to view on the internet using a web browser.

Notes:

In each section throughout the book, you will be required to add new lines of code. Each new line of code in each section will be highlighted in red.

For Example:

```
<!doctype html>
<HTML>
<head>
   <meta charset="utf-8">
   <title>Planet Splendor</title>
</head>
<body>
</body>
</HTML>
```

 This is the new line of code that you would need to add.

By the end of the book, you'll have your website on your personal device but it will not be available for public viewing.

The QuestKids™ series is an imprint of In Easy Steps Limited
16 Hamilton Terrace • Holly Walk • Leamington Spa •
Warwickshire • United Kingdom • CV32 4LY
www.ineasysteps.com

ISBN: 978-1-84078-828-0

Notice of Liability
Every effort has been made to ensure that this book contains accurate and current information. However, In Easy Steps Limited and the authors shall not be liable for any loss or damage suffered by readers as a result of any information contained herein.

MIX
Paper from
responsible sources
FSC
www.fsc.org   FSC® C020837

Printed and bound in the United Kingdom

Contributors
Technical Author: Darryl Bartlett
Designer & Illustrator: Ben Barter
Story Author: Paul Aldridge

Contents Page:

You can download the full source code for the book from
http://www.thequestkids.com

"Wow!!!" gasped Dan.

"That! Ah, that's just one of our regular shuttle flights," replied Uncle Pimlico as they all walked towards the Space Center. "Now! It's a big day for us here today. So... I need you on your best behavior."

"Always, Uncle!" replied Tiff. "Same for you, hey Dan?" Tiff nudged him and winked as he slowly understood.

"Oh, erm... absolutely! As if we weren't even here," replied Dan.

"Doubtful... and your plans for them?" Uncle Pimlico stared at Smuffy and Chew-Chew. "I still haven't forgiven that chinchilla for the last time it escaped and chased me!"

"All sorted. I've added a lock to Chew-Chew's ball," replied Tiff.

"... and I'll take Smuffy when, you know... she has to go out," said Dan.

"Excellent!" yelled Uncle Pimlico. They walked on through the entrance and eventually came to a standstill, spellbound by the enormous atrium.

"Wow!" exclaimed Dan and Tiff as they looked around.

"Can we wander?" asked Dan.

"No, no, no!" snapped Uncle Pimlico. "Although, here's the deal. If you behave, I'll take you on an amazing tour in a spaceship."

"Deal!" they replied excitedly. Everyone strolled on until Uncle Pimlico stopped abruptly. A sliding door with swirling neon lights faced them.

"Right, kids. We're about to enter the Nerve Center for this entire complex. Follow me and don't touch anything! Understood?" he asked.

They both sneakily crossed their fingers. "We promise," they replied.

"Same goes for you two!" Uncle Pimlico stared at their pets. "Okay gang, let's go!"

SPACE CENTER

As they walked in, the room came alive. Neon lights lit up, monitors powered on, and machines hummed and whirred.

Dan's eyes widened. "You must have such an important job, Mr Pimlico?"

"Well... yes! I guess so," he replied, "although if today doesn't go well I may need a new one."

"What's so special about today, Uncle?" asked Tiff.

"Why don't I show you?" Uncle Pimlico tapped on his device. Suddenly, laser beams flashed from all angles, creating an illuminated sphere in the center of the room.

"This... is Planet Splendor! It's in our next Galaxy." Uncle Pimlico stood back and marveled at the hologram. "It will be a lot like Earth, only better!"

"Did you build it, Uncle?" asked Tiff.

"Me? No, my part is to design the website that powers everything with clean, renewable energy sourced from crystallized moisture particles

found in the air. It's all rather top secret, you know!" he said as he tapped the side of his nose with his finger. Suddenly, a monitor crackled loudly as a distorted image slowly appeared and a garbled voice sounded out, "Pimlico! My office. Now!"

"Sir? Oh yes, sir! Right away." Uncle Pimlico stepped back. "That was my boss. I'll have to go and see him straightaway. Now, erm... kids. I need you to stay here. Don't leave this room and don't touch anything. Remember your promise."

Tiff half-smiled before she answered. "What could we get up to in a place like this, Uncle?"

"Exactly! I'll be back very soon. We launch in an hour." As he raced out he began to mutter to himself, "Hmm. I hope my boss is okay? He didn't sound too good."

Dan and Tiff stood silently, gazing around the room. "Ready?" asked Tiff.

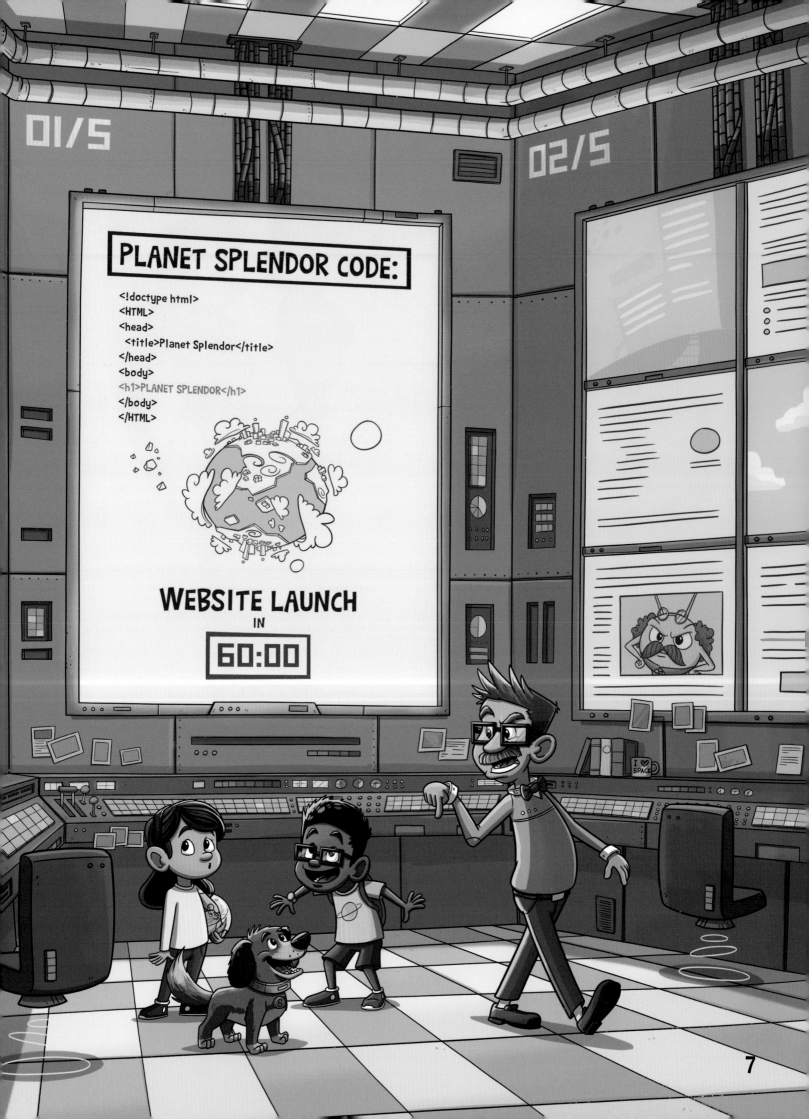

Dan looked around. "What shall we not touch first?"

"How about that 4D printer over there," replied Tiff, smiling. Suddenly, the sliding door swooshed open. In the doorway stood a very odd-looking Caretaker.

"What are you two doing in here?" he asked.

"My Uncle works here. He's very important!" explained Tiff.

The Caretaker edged towards them. "Well, I need you gone. I gotta clean up this mess and I don't need kids getting under my feet!"

"But, but..." cried Tiff.

"But nothing!" interrupted the Caretaker. "Shoo! Come back when I'm done. Stay any longer and I'll take my mop to you... take those beasts as well!"

"Let's go, Dan. This guy's crazy!" said Tiff as they left the room. The Caretaker was now alone. He reached inside his overalls, pulled out some papers and began to type.

The screen flashed with page after page of coding.

"You're mine now!" he roared as he pressed Print. Paper churned through the printer and he quickly gathered it up in joy. As he did, Smuffy suddenly popped up. They stared long and hard at each other. Smuffy began to growl as the petrified Caretaker retreated. His left arm slowly reached up as his fingers searched the keyboard. Smuffy inched forward and bared her teeth.

"Got you!" the Caretaker shouted as he pressed a key, jumped up and scarpered. The screens began to flash wildly. Smuffy turned away and spotted the Caretaker almost at the door. He leapt up and Smuffy scampered after him. The Caretaker suddenly realized he had Smuffy snapping at his heels.

"No!!!!!!!!!!!!!!" he screamed as he raced out the door.

Smuffy was inching closer when the Caretaker's disguise began to unravel. Firstly his cap then his moustache flew off, revealing a little green face. Smuffy swerved left and right, trying to avoid them as they sprinted towards Dan and Tiff.

"What's that noise?" asked Dan as they span around. With a mighty whoosh, chaos flew past them.

"Hey! That's the Caretaker! Where's he going?" yelled Dan.

"...and why is Smuffy chasing him?" asked Tiff.

Suddenly, Chew-Chew jumped up. His ball flew through the air and split into two as it landed.

"Oh dear! He's in trouble now!" said Tiff as Chew-Chew flashed his razor-sharp gnashers and dashed after the Caretaker.

As the Caretaker sprinted, he could sense the two animals gaining closer and closer on him. He rapidly approached the door and bashed straight through it, accidentally dropping a piece of paper. His pursuers drew alongside each other and prepared to attack. Dan and Tiff ran as far as the door, then stood and watched, utterly bewildered, through the window as their pets closed in. Suddenly, they pounced!

"Arghhhhhhhhhhhhhhhhh!!!!" shouted the Caretaker.

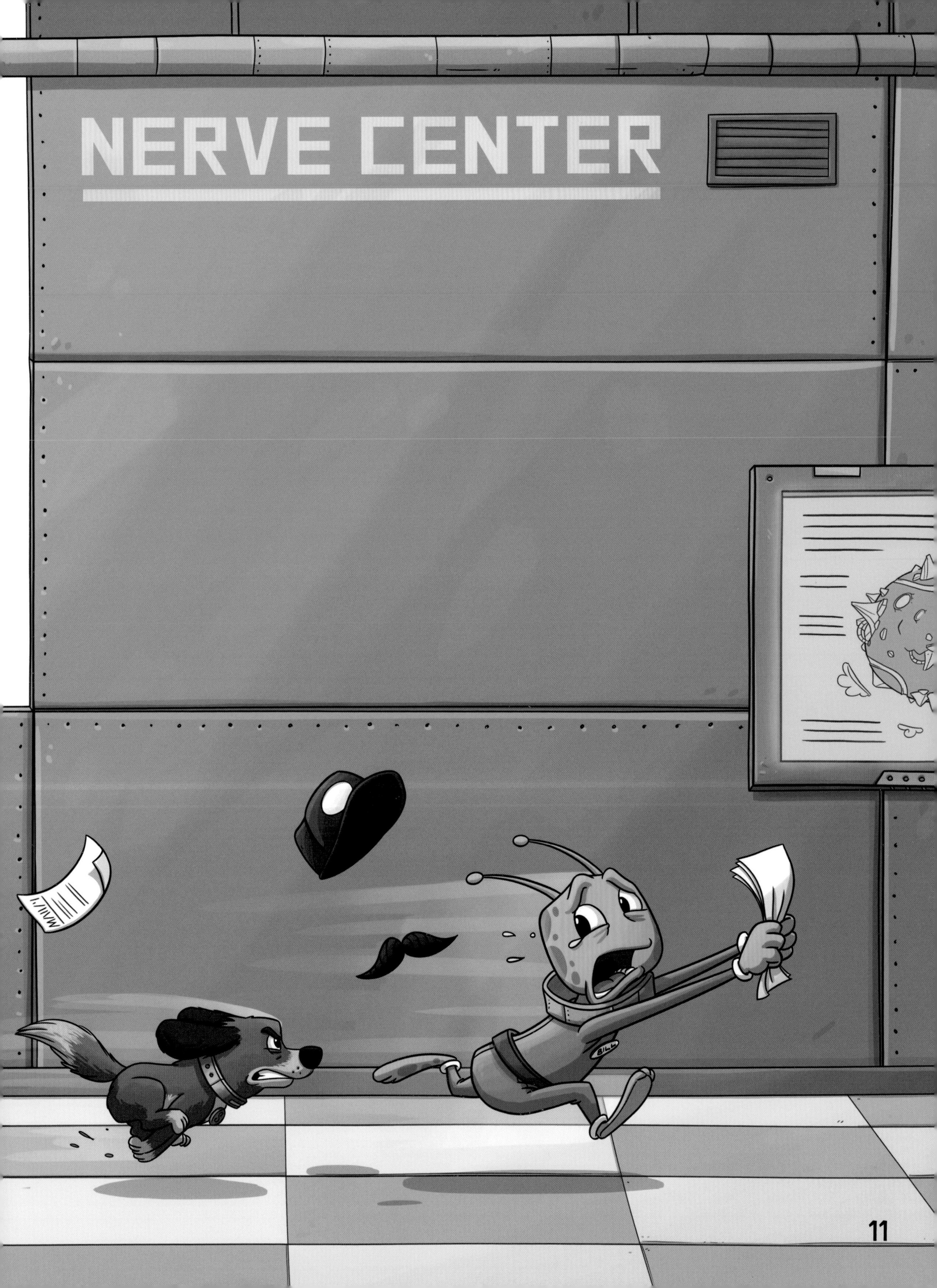
NERVE CENTER
BILL

Smuffy and Chew-Chew leapt up and sank their teeth into the Caretaker's overalls. As they did, they ripped a section clean off. The Caretaker somehow kept his balance and carried on running towards a battered old spaceship on the landing pad. A group of other green characters stood waving him in.

The pets were so busy tearing into the material that they hadn't noticed the figure had escaped into the ship. Suddenly, the ground began to shake and smoke poured out as the craft began to lift. Slow, at first, then rapidly accelerating as it spluttered and stuttered into the sky. Dan and Tiff watched, mesmerized.

"What just happened?" asked Dan. "...and how did that Caretaker become an alien?"

"There were a whole group of aliens... and in an old spacecraft, Dan!" replied Tiff sarcastically.

"I know that, but what were they doing here?" queried Dan.

"That bit I don't know," said Tiff, "but I'm about to find out!" With that, she turned towards the Nerve Center. "Come on Dan, we need to find out what the alien was doing." Dan grabbed Smuffy and Chew-Chew and turned to follow. Dan picked up the dropped page. He could only just make out the word Masterplan. "What's that?" he asked.

"It must be the reason why the alien was here," replied Tiff. "The answers have to be in that Nerve Center. Let's go." They raced back in and were greeted by completely blank screens.

"Where's all the code gone?" asked Dan.

"I'd best find out!" replied Tiff as she typed frantically. "I think he's printed off the code before deleting it all from this computer!"

"But that means your Uncle can't launch the site," yelled Dan, "and that countdown clock is ticking!"

"I know! Give me a minute. Let me think!" said Tiff. She opened file after file on the screen and hurriedly typed. Within a minute she suddenly stopped. "That's it. I have it!" she exclaimed. "Everyone gather round."

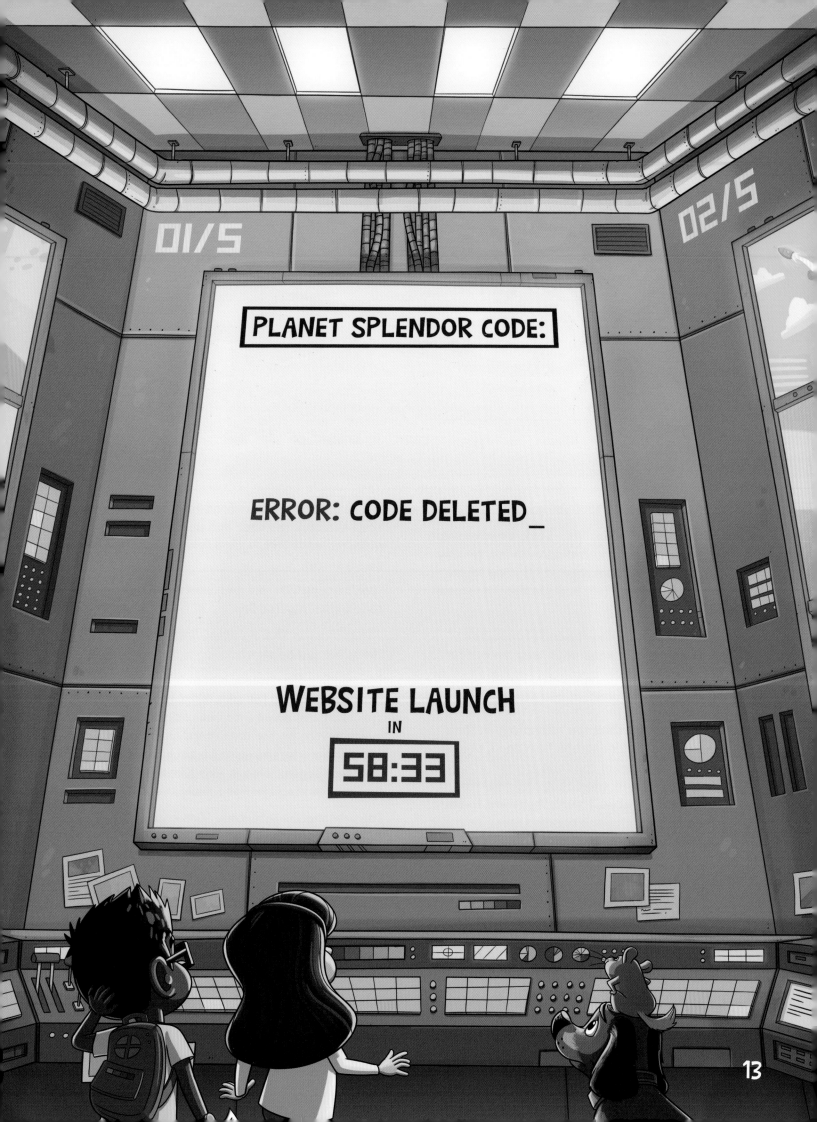

Tiff span round to face the group.

"I have a plan!" said Tiff. "Look, we have their masterplan and I'm already tracking the ship using the data from here so I'll know where they're heading." Tiff brought another screen online.

"They've only stolen the code for Uncle's website, so they knew what they were after. We also know that the Caretaker wasn't alone. From the security cameras, I've matched all the aliens with the profiles in the database. I've also researched the technology in their Galaxy and they're so old-fashioned, which is why they needed the code printed off. Now they have Uncle's code, they could become far more advanced. I think they want to build their own website and create a new planet for themselves!" Tiff paused.

"That's brilliant, Tiff! What can we do to stop them?" asked Dan.

"We need to go and get the code back!" said Tiff.

"Leave it to me... and I have just the right spaceship." yelled Dan. "Let's go, Smuffy!"

"We'll stay here and defend the Nerve Center. You send back the code and we'll rebuild the website," said Tiff. "...And Dan, we have to keep this a secret."

"Don't worry Tiff, me and Smuffy will get that code back!" replied Dan.

"That clock is ticking down, Dan," warned Tiff. "Be quick, but be careful."

Dan and Smuffy raced towards the launch pad. They jumped into the spaceship, grabbed a spacesuit and dived into the cockpit. Dan pushed every button on the dashboard until suddenly, the engines started up and a countdown sequence began. "This is just like a video game!" Dan said as they strapped themselves in.

Dan pressed the intercom. "Come in, Tiff."

"Receiving!" replied Tiff.

"We're ready for launch. Let's catch some aliens!" said Dan. "Three... two... one... lift off. QuestKids away!!!!!!!!!!!!!!!!"

Dan's spaceship thundered into the cosmos, following the trail of the alien craft.

"Tiff... come in?" said Dan.

"Hi, Dan. I've got you on screen," replied Tiff. "You're still a distance from them, but they're also nearing a planet which I'm just ID-ing."

"Any update on who they are?" asked Dan.

"I'm just transmitting a file," replied Tiff. "Pull up the data when it arrives."

"Got it!" said Dan as he displayed the data on screen.

"The alien who pretended to be the Caretaker calls himself Emperor Ibebot from the Planet Chillico. I bet he's the leader of this group of alien nitwits," said Tiff. "Weirdly, though, they're flying towards Planet Shumko, which is the home planet of the Zeeogs. There must be a Zeeog on the spaceship with them."

Okay, Tiff. I think I can see the planet ahead, said Dan.

"I've started to rebuild the website," replied Tiff. "Well at least with the basic coding that I know, but without those pages..."

Dan interrupted. "Don't worry, we'll get you that code!"

"Just so you know, Dan, this planet is the recycling junkyard of their Galaxy. The Zeeogs love playing games but are famous for their stupidity."

"We have something in common then!" joked Dan as he pressed the booster rockets. "Over and out." Dan seized the controls. "Right, Smuffy... Planet Shumko for us."

Emperor Ibebot held out the pages of code and began to divide them into three. He handed round the pages to Lord Zeeog and Sultan Tromot, who instantly dropped them. "Ah! Pick them up, you idiot. Now, you know what to do with them?" asked Emperor Ibebot.

"I will give it to my best coders," replied Sultan Tromot anxiously.

"Hey? Oh... erm. Our section will be ready," said Lord Zeeog nervously.

"Magnificent," Ibebot said. "When we upload our separate sections we will create a master website that even that Earthling, Pimlico, would be proud of. Then, we'll create our own new planet and wave goodbye to our wastelands." The alien leader rubbed his hands together and grinned.

"Now, get ready to land on your own planet," he said, "and remember, I'm sure those pesky QuestKids will be chasing us by now so look out for them... and especially that dog! You know how much I hate anything canine... and whatever happens, do not give them this code!" Ibebot pressed a few buttons and landed on Planet Shumko. "Out!" he shouted as he shoved the small alien Zeeog out of the escape hatch and took off.

Moments later, Dan came in to land and scanned the area for signs of life. It was strangely quiet as they both jumped out and began to look around. From the top of the hill they could see two beaten-up robots that looked like they had been in a war. "Ah! Combat Bots. Let's investigate, Smuffy," whispered Dan.

The silence was broken when the small alien, Lord Zeeog, appeared out of nowhere with his robot bodyguards.

"I was hoping never to meet you, Dan Devices," the alien said in a wobbly voice. "I'm Lord Zeeog and you have no business here."

"I do!" said Dan. "You have something that doesn't belong to you... and I'm here to get it back!"

"Really! What's your plan? After all, there's just you and that... thing! Whereas I have a team of deadly robots at my command," he said.

"Hmm," Dan looked around, "how about I play you at... Combat Bots? If I win, you hand me the code. If I lose you get my..."

"Spaceship!" interrupted the Lord. "I'll enjoy converting it into a champion Bot!"

Dan paused for a few seconds. "Deal! Let's battle!"

They all stood around the edge of a clearing. The robot bodyguards wheeled out two Combat Bots.

"This is mine," said the Lord, "...and that one is yours!" Dan stared at the heap of old junk. "Hmm. What shall I turn your ship into?" said the Lord as his Super-Bot raced around. Dan's Bot barely moved. "Let's battle!" shouted the Lord.

Suddenly, the huge Bot ploughed into Dan's, scattering pieces everywhere. It reversed and rushed forward again, knocking chunks off its rival. Dan desperately moved his controls and limped away. "We'll need a miracle here, Smuffy!" said Dan. "Any ideas?"

Lord Zeeog cheered as a huge rotating disc appeared from his Combat Bot's telescopic arm. Its engine revved as it accelerated forward. Suddenly, Dan's Bot dodged to the left. As it did,

the Lord's Bot veered towards Smuffy. She bounded into the air and landed on Dan, who dropped his controller. As Smuffy recovered, she accidentally pressed a button on Dan's wrist-tech band. Their Bot suddenly span out of control and smashed viciously into its opponent. Both arms tore into the metal, as sparks and smoke billowed out. Lord Zeeog fell silent in shock.

"Well, that was easy!" said Dan. "Code, please?" Lord Zeeog, still in shock, fumbled around and held out a page. "All of it!" said Dan.

"Here," replied the defeated Lord. Dan and Smuffy ran back to their spaceship, jumped in and fired up the rockets. "Top work, Smuffy. Let's fly!" shouted Dan. Dan blasted off in search of the other two aliens, leaving the Lord starring at his broken battle Bot in despair.

Dan quickly got on the intercom while sending the data he had retrieved, "Hey Tiff, you there?"

"Hey Dan," she replied, "anything for me?"

"You'd best get typing! Have a look on your screen," said Dan.

"How did you get it back?" asked Tiff.

"Smuffy gave them the runaround," joked Dan.

Tiff downloaded the data and began to type. "Brilliant, Dan. I'm coding as we speak!"

"Where next?" he asked.

Planet Dealrn! It's home to the Tromots," said Tiff. "I'm sending the profiles and co-ordinates now."

"How is everything back in the Nerve Center?" asked Dan.

"So far, so good," said Tiff, "Chew-Chew is guarding the door while I code, and now he seems to be building a small trebuchet!"

"Guarding doors is the perfect job for that lunatic chinchilla!" laughed Dan.

Tiff nodded in agreement. "You got that right!"

Follow the next few pages to create your first website with The QuestKids!

Learn how to get started and how to edit your webpages.
Add headings, titles, tables and links to your webpages.

Getting Started

To get started with HTML, we need to set up the standard HTML document structure.

1 Open up your text editor and type out the code below:

```
<!doctype html>
<HTML>
<head>
  <meta charset="utf-8">
  <title></title>
</head>
<body>
</body>
</HTML>
```

Remember to note down the location of your document.

2 Save the document as planet.html.

Try to save it in a memorable location, like on the Desktop or in the Documents folder.

Viewing Your Webpage

You can view your webpage at anytime throughout the book by double-clicking the planet.html file.

1 Browse Windows Explorer on PC or Finder on Mac for planet.html.

Your document will still be blank at this stage. However, this is how the final website will look.

2 Double-click on planet.html, and the page will open in your default web browser.

Editing Your Webpage

Throughout the book, you will need to add more code to complete the project. You can edit your webpage at any point by following the steps below:

1 Open your chosen text editor (Notepad, Sublime Text, etc.).

We recommend using Sublime Text for writing code.

You can get it from here: **sublimetext.com**

2 Select planet.html to open the document in your text editor.

Make sure you are using a plain text editor, and not a word processor like Microsoft Word.

Headings and Page Titles

Adding a Title

We are going to start by giving our page a title. We do this using the <title> tag. A page title is not printed on the page itself, but instead it's displayed in the browser toolbar. This title would also be displayed in the search engine results.

1 Add the following line of code to your document:

```
<!doctype html>
<HTML>
<head>
  <meta charset="utf-8">
  <title>Planet Splendor</title>
</head>
<body>
</body>
</HTML>
```

2 Save the changes to your document, by clicking File > Save.

Adding a Heading

Next, we will add a nice big header to the top of the page. This will be printed at the very top of the webpage.

1 Add the following line of code inside your <body> tag:

```
<!doctype html>
<HTML>
<head>
  <meta charset="utf-8">
  <title>Planet Splendor</title>
</head>
<body>
  <h1>PLANET SPLENDOR</h1>
</body>
</HTML>
```

2 Save the changes to your document, by clicking File > Save. Your webpage should now look like the screenshot below:

Remember to close off tags to avoid problems with your code.

For the <title> opening tag, you would use </title> as the closing tag.

PLANET SPLENDOR

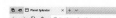

Paragraphs

You can also use the <br> tag to create a line break in your paragraph.

All websites contain some form of text. We are going to use the <p> tag to create a paragraph of text for our page.

1 Add the following lines of code to your document:

```
<!doctype html>
<HTML>
<head>
   <meta charset="utf-8">
   <title>Planet Splendor</title>
</head>
<body>
   <h1>PLANET SPLENDOR</h1>
   <p>This website was created using HTML from 'The QuestKids do
   Coding – Create Your First Website in easy steps' book. This is Planet
   Splendor. By launching this website it will upload the power needed
   to run the entire planet. This new world has the perfect climate, with
   renewable energy, no pollution, rubbish is banned, in a place where
   everyone gets along. A planet like no other, where everything in your
   imagination is already there.</p>
</body>
</HTML>
```

2 Save the changes to your document, by clicking File > Save. Your webpage should now look like the screenshot below:

This website was created using HTML from 'The QuestKids do Coding – Create Your First Website in easy steps' book. This is Planet Splendor. By launching this website it will upload the power needed to run the entire planet. This new world has the perfect climate, with renewable energy, no pollution, rubbish is banned, in a place where everyone gets along. A planet like no other, where everything in your imagination is already there.

Images

We need to make our webpage more appealing, so we are now going to add an image of a planet to the webpage. The img src tag allows us to do that. Add the following lines of code to your document:

img stands for image.

src stands for source. This tells the browser where to look for the image.

An alt attribute is used to tell the browser what text to render
if there is a problem locating the image.

1 Add the following line of code to your document:

```
<!doctype html>
<HTML>
<head>
  <meta charset="utf-8">
  <title>Planet Splendor</title>
</head>
<body>
  <h1>PLANET SPLENDOR</h1>
  <p>This website was created using HTML from 'The QuestKids do
  Coding – Create Your First Website in easy steps' book. This is Planet
  Splendor. By launching this website it will upload the power needed
  to run the entire planet. This new world has the perfect climate, with
  renewable energy, no pollution, rubbish is banned, in a place where
  everyone gets along. A planet like no other, where everything in your
  imagination is already there.</p>
  <img src="http://www.thequestkids.com/planetsplendor.png"
  alt="Planet">
</body>
</HTML>
```

2 Save the changes to your document, by clicking File > Save. Your webpage should now look like the screenshot below:

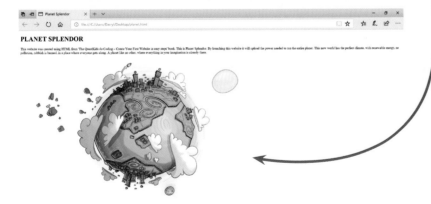

Tables

We will now add some more images and text to our page. However, this time we will be using a table to display them. Tables are a good way of structuring data, and are mainly used for text. In this instance, we will be adding an icon along with some text in each row.

1 Add the following lines in red below to create a table. This will go underneath the image we created on the previous page.

```
<body>
   ...
<h1>PLANET SPLENDOR</h1>
<p>This website was created using HTML from 'The QuestKids do
Coding – Create Your First Website in easy steps' book. This is Planet
Splendor. By launching this website it will upload the power needed to
run the entire planet. This new world has the perfect climate, with
renewable energy, no pollution, rubbish is banned, in a place where
everyone gets along. A planet like no other, where everything in your
imagination is already there.</p>
<img src="http://www.thequestkids.com/planetsplendor.png"
alt="Planet">
<table>
  <tr>
    <td><img src="http://www.thequestkids.com/iconcity.png"
    alt="Cities"></td>
    <td>Awesome cities, towns and homes</td>
  </tr>
  <tr>
    <td><img src="http://www.thequestkids.com/iconforest.png"
    alt="Forests"></td>
    <td>Beautiful forests, lakes, oceans and mountainscapes</td>
  </tr>
  <tr>
    <td><img src="http://www.thequestkids.com/iconweather.png"
    alt="Weather"></td>
    <td>Amazing weather and wildlife</td>
  </tr>
  <tr>
    <td><img src="http://www.thequestkids.com/iconenergy.png"
    alt="Energy"></td>
    <td>Renewable Energy</td>
  </tr>
  <tr>
    <td><img src="http://www.thequestkids.com/icontech.png"
    alt="Technology"></td>
    <td>Flying cars and new technology</td>
  </tr>
</table>
</body>
</HTML>
```

Continued ...

An ellipsis (...) in the blue code section means some of the code from an earlier section is not repeated here. Remember, you just need to focus on the code in red. Add this red code as shown here.

Make sure that you keep links on the same line to avoid any problems with the file/media location. This is especially important with the <img> and <link> tags.

If you are struggling with the positioning of any of the code in the book, then you can always review the final source code on pages 66-68 to see where the code needs to go.

... Tables Continued

We use the <table> tag to begin creating our table.

<tr> stands for table row. This sets up a new row.

<td> stands for table data. This is where we would add our text or image.

We have created 5 rows with 2 lots of data images in each row (an image and a piece of text).

🏠 Awesome cities, towns and homes

🌳 Beautiful forests, lakes, oceans and mountainscapes

☀ Amazing weather and wildlife

⚡ Renewable Energy

💡 Flying cars and new technology

For more advanced tables, you can use tags like <caption>, <thead> and <tbody>.

2 Save the changes to your document, by clicking File > Save.
Your webpage should now look like the screenshot below:

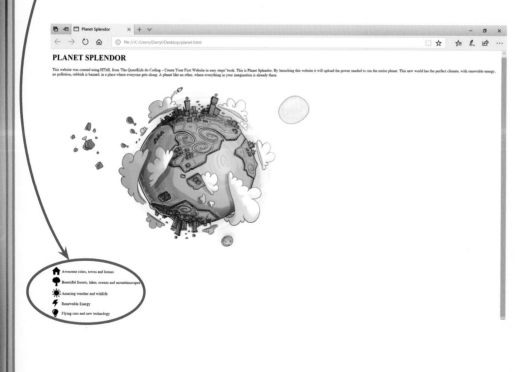

Lists

We will now create a list of items on our webpage. This will include your name, today's date, etc. To do this we will be using the <ul> tag. This creates an unordered list. Each item in the list will have an <li> tag next to it, which simply marks it as one of the items being listed. All items will be displayed in bullet points.

1 Add the following lines of code underneath the </table> tag:

```
...
    </tr>
  </table>
  <ul>
    <li>Creator:</li>
    <li>Launched:</li>
    <li>Planet Origin:</li>
    <li>Species:</li>
    <li>Age:</li>
  </ul>
...
```

2 You will notice in the last step we just added Creator, Launched, Planet Origin, etc. without adding any extra details. Under "Creator", you will want to put your own name. You will also want to add your own age and today's date. Feel free to add in your own details, or use the code below:

```
<ul>
    <li>Creator: Dan</li>
    <li>Launched: 7th December</li>
    <li>Planet Origin: Earth</li>
    <li>Species: Human</li>
    <li>Age: 10</li>
</ul>
```

3 Save the changes to your document, by clicking File > Save. Your webpage should now display a list similar to the one in the screenshot below:

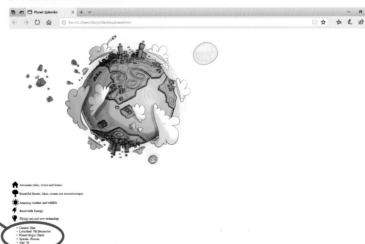

- Creator: Dan
- Launched: 7th December
- Planet Origin: Earth
- Species: Human
- Age: 10

Links

Most websites will contain links to other pages. We are going to create our own link at the bottom of the page in the form of a copyright notice. This will link back to The QuestKids website. To create a link, we use the <a> tag. We will place this inside a footer, which is what usually goes at the bottom of the page.

① Add the following line of code underneath the list we just created:

```
<head>
...
</head>
<body>
  <h1>PLANET SPLENDOR</h1>
  <p>...</p>
  <img src="http://www.thequestkids.com/planetsplendor.png"
  alt="Planet">
  <table>
    <tr>
      <td><img src="http://www.thequestkids.com/iconcity.png"
      alt="Cities"></td>
      <td>Awesome cities, towns and homes</td>
    </tr>
    <tr>
      <td><img src="http://www.thequestkids.com/iconforest.png"
      alt="Forests"></td>
      <td>Beautiful forests, lakes, oceans and mountainscapes</td>
    </tr>
    <tr>
      <td><img src="http://www.thequestkids.com/
      iconweather.png" alt="Weather"></td>
      <td>Amazing weather and wildlife</td>
    </tr>
    <tr>
      <td><img src="http://www.thequestkids.com/iconenergy.png"
      alt="Energy"></td>
      <td>Renewable Energy</td>
    </tr>
    <tr>
      <td><img src="http://www.thequestkids.com/icontech.png"
      alt="Technology"></td>
      <td>Flying cars and new technology</td>
    </tr>
  </table>
  <ul>
  ...
  </ul>
  <a href="http://www.thequestkids.com">The QuestKids</a>
</body>
</HTML>
```

Hot tip

A link doesn't always have to be text. You can use an image and many other HTML elements.

▶▶ Continued ...

... Links Continued

The <a> tag allows us to create a link from one page to another. The href attribute is where you would put the link address. In this case, it's http://www.thequestkids.com.

The text afterwards, which says "The QuestKids", is how the link will appear on the page.

2 Save the changes to your document, by clicking File > Save. You should now see your link right at the bottom of the page.

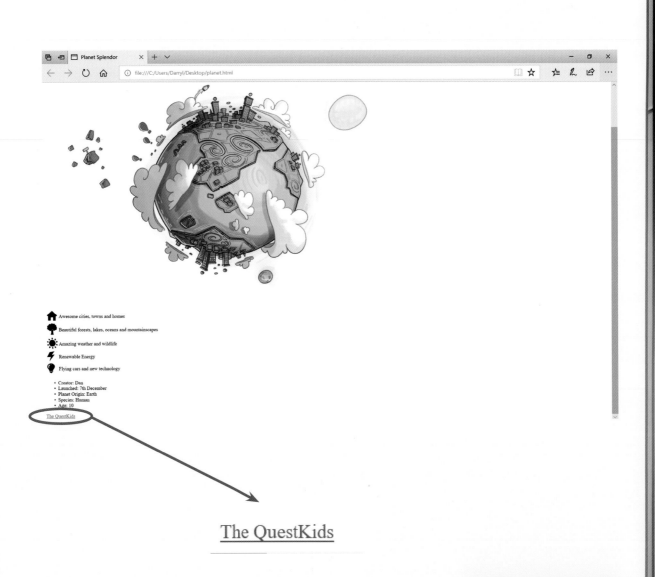

The QuestKids

Back to the adventure...

The spaceship blasted across the sky as Dan looked at the rocky desert below. In the distance, he could just make out some menacing figures.

"Aha! Tromots!" he said.

Dan searched for a place to land, eventually finding an ideal spot. Below, a group of Tromots were kicking around a boulder in a makeshift game of football. As the spaceship descended, its engines blasted away the ball and all remnants of the pitch. Gradually the dust settled. The now angry and curious Tromots gathered by the rocket and waited for the door to open.

"You landed, Dan?" asked Tiff.

"Well I've landed on something," he replied.

Tiff prepared the bad news. "Tromots are the ogres of their Galaxy... they're strong, stupid, and not very friendly. But at least their air is breathable so you won't need your helmets."

"Well... if it's the aliens I'm looking at, it's definitely them!" joked Dan. "And... it looks like there's no welcome party." Dan smiled at them through the window.

"Erm... you go first this time, Smuffy!"

PLANET DEARTH

"You ruined our game," yelled Sultan Tromot. "We were 2-1 up!"

"If you give me the code back... I'll let you get on," replied Dan.

"Nothing for you here apart from dust!" The Sultan's guards gathered round.

"Fortunately for you, I was taught some manners. Can I have the code back... please?" said Dan politely.

"Manners won't help either!" The Sultan paused and looked down at Smuffy. "Actually, I've always wanted a little pooch. How about a trade? Come to Daddy!"

"Ermmm!" Smuffy stared at Dan with a worried look. "I'll play you for her?" Dan said, winking at Smuffy.

"You've no chance," the Sultan laughed. "We'll play our favorite game here."

"What's that?" asked Dan.

"Watch!" The Sultan said as he walked over to a boulder. He bent down, picked it up and flung it in the direction of Dan. "Stone tossing! Your turn, puny one." Dan looked around. As he did, he remembered a device on his wrist-tech band.

"Hmm, that one," said Dan as he confidently walked over to a massive boulder. "Jump on, Smuffy!"

The Tromots began to chuckle as Dan crouched down behind the rock. Now hidden, he looked at his wrist-tech band and pressed the Anti-gravity button. Suddenly, an invisible phaser beam surrounded the boulder. Dan pretended to struggle slightly as he lifted it way above his head. The Tromots gasped and stood back. "Jump off, Smuffy!" said Dan calmly as he launched the boulder. As everyone looked on, Dan secretly pressed the button, making the rock fall to the ground.

"I win!" said Dan. "Now, where's that code?" The Sultan stood nervously. Smuffy bounded forward and snarled, causing the Sultan to fall backwards towards the others. As he fell into them, they began to tumble like dominoes, eventually creating a huge tower of Tromots. As they balanced precariously, a piece of paper floated in the air.

"Grab it!" shouted Dan as Smuffy jumped up and caught it between her teeth. "Spaceship! Now!" he bellowed as they sped across the ground and hurled themselves in.

It didn't take long before Dan and Smuffy had launched and blasted safely into space. "Who would have known I was so strong?" smiled Dan.

"Dan! Code, code, code?" yelled Tiff.

"All yours! Transmitting now," replied Dan.

"Was he easy to convince?" she asked.

"Ah, we just chucked some stones about!" he said.

"Hope you're joking," replied Tiff.

"Don't worry Tiff... just get coding!" said Dan.

She downloaded the code and began to type furiously, switching rapidly between screens. As she did, she noticed on the security monitor Uncle Pimlico walking back towards the Nerve Center.

"How are we doing for time?" asked Dan.

"Oh dear, this is not good!" Tiff snapped.

"What?! What?!" Dan replied, slightly worried by the sound of Tiff's voice. Dan listened as he could hear Tiff having a conversation with Chew-Chew.

"Chew-Chew! He's coming back... what can we do? What are you looking for on the computer? How did you gain access into the Space Center's building controls!? We can't lock him in the elevator, Chew-Chew!?" cried Tiff.

"Do it, Tiff!" Dan shouted. "It will only be for a short while. We need more time."

"I guess you're both right. Okay, it's done. He will be locked in the elevator for a little while, Dan, so you'd better get a move on. Listen... this was an accident, okay Dan?" Tiff said, feeling very guilty about locking her uncle in an elevator.

"Of course, Tiff." Dan giggled.

"You too, Chew-Chew!" said Tiff. "It was an accident, okay. Never squeak a word!"

Now, you can work on your page structure, and allow visitors to your site to navigate around various pages.

36

Page Structure

We have now added some basic HTML elements to our page. However, if you look at the page in its current form, you will notice the page isn't structured very well. It's all running down one side of the page. Also, if you look at the page on a mobile device, it doesn't look that great at all.

We are now going to use a front-end component library called Bootstrap to give our page a much better structure.

❶ First of all, we need to add a reference to the Bootstrap library. We can do this inside the <head></head> tags. Add the following line of code underneath the title:

```
<!doctype html>
<HTML>
<head>
   <title>Planet Splendor</title>
   <link rel="stylesheet" href="https://maxcdn.bootstrapcdn.com/
   bootstrap/3.3.7/css/bootstrap.min.css">
</head>
<body>
   <h1>PLANET SPLENDOR</h1>
   <p>This website was created using HTML from 'The QuestKids do
   Coding – Create Your First Website in easy steps' book. This is Planet
   Splendor. By launching this website it will upload the power needed
   to run the entire planet. This new world has the perfect climate, with
   renewable energy, no pollution, rubbish is banned, in a place where
   everyone gets along. A planet like no other, where everything in your
   imagination is already there.</p>
   <img src="http://www.thequestkids.com/planetsplendor.png"
   alt="Planet">
   <table>
   <tr>
   ...
   </tr>
   </table>
   <ul>
     <li>Creator: Dan</li>
     <li>Launched: 7th December</li>
     <li>Planet Origin: Earth</li>
     <li>Species: Human</li>
     <li>Age: 10</li>
   </ul>
   <a href="http://www.thequestkids.com">The QuestKids</a>
</body>
</HTML>
```

You can find out more about Bootstrap by going to: **getbootstrap.com**

Make sure that you keep links on the same line to avoid any problems with the file/media location. This is especially important with the <img> and <link> tags.

Continued ...

... Page Structure Continued

If you are struggling with the positioning of any of the code in the book, then you can always review the final source code on pages 66-68 to see where the code needs to go.

2 We are now going to surround the content we have created with tags called <div class=" ">. This allows us to assign styles to each area. We will be creating our own styles a little later on, but for now we will use ones that have been set up by Bootstrap. Add the following red lines of code:

```html
<body>
<div class="container-fluid">
  <h1>PLANET SPLENDOR</h1>
  <div class="row">
    <div class="col-md-12">
    <p>This website was created using HTML from 'The QuestKids
    do Coding – Create Your First Website in easy steps' book. This is
    Planet Splendor. By launching this website it will upload the power
    needed to run the entire planet. This new world has the perfect
    climate, with renewable energy, no pollution, rubbish is banned, in
    a place where everyone gets along. A planet like no other, where
    everything in your imagination is already there.</p>
    </div>
  </div>
    <table>
      <tr>
        <td><img src="http://www.thequestkids.com/iconcity.png"
        alt="Cities"></td>
        <td>Awesome cities, towns and homes</td>
      </tr>
      <tr>
        <td><img src="http://www.thequestkids.com/iconforest.png"
        alt="Forests"></td>
        <td>Beautiful forests, lakes, oceans and mountainscapes</td>
      </tr>
      <tr>
        <td><img src="http://www.thequestkids.com/
        iconweather.png" alt="Weather"></td>
        <td>Amazing weather and wildlife</td>
      </tr>
      <tr>
        <td><img src="http://www.thequestkids.com/iconenergy.png"
        alt="Energy"></td>
        <td>Renewable Energy</td>
      </tr>
      <tr>
        <td><img src="http://www.thequestkids.com/icontech.png"
        alt="Technology"></td>
        <td>Flying cars and new technology</td>
      </tr>
    </table>
```

 Continued ...

... Page Structure Continued

```
<ul>
  <li>Creator: Dan</li>
  <li>Launched: 7th December</li>
  <li>Planet Origin: Earth</li>
  <li>Species: Human</li>
  <li>Age: 10</li>
</ul>
<a href="http://www.thequestkids.com">The QuestKids</a>
</div>
</body>
```

First of all, we have set up a div class called <div class="container-fluid">. This Bootstrap class provides a full-width container for our content.

We have then surrounded our paragraph of text with a div class called row and another div class called col-md-12.

<div class = "row"> – The "row" class is used to hold columns. Bootstrap divides each row into a grid of 12 virtual columns.

<div class = "col-md-12"> – This will make the width of the content 100%.

You will notice we close off divisions with </div>. This stops this class being assigned to anything else after that point.

3 We will now assign a <footer> tag to our link as well. A footer is the content that appears at the bottom of the page. Let's add the following code:

```
<body>
  ...
  <ul>
    <li>Creator: Dan</li>
    <li>Launched: 7th December</li>
    <li>Planet Origin: Earth</li>
    <li>Species: Human</li>
    <li>Age: 10</li>
  </ul>
  <footer>
    <a href="http://www.thequestkids.com">The QuestKids</a>
  </footer>
</div>
</body>
</HTML>
```

An ellipsis (...) in the blue code section means some of the code from an earlier section is not repeated here. Remember, you just need to focus on the code in red. Add this red code as shown here.

Continued ...

... Page Structure Continued

Beware

Once Bootstrap has been added to the project, it will start adding its own styles to the elements.

④ We will now assign the style col-md-6 to a few areas of our code. col-md-6 will make each area 50%, so that the page is split up into two. Let's add the following code:

```
<body>
<div class="container-fluid">
  <h1>PLANET SPLENDOR</h1>
  <div class="row">
    <div class="col-md-12">
      <p>...</p>
    </div>
  </div>
  <div class="row">
    <div class="col-md-6">
      <img src="http://www.thequestkids.com/planetsplendor.png"
      alt="Planet">
    </div>
    <div class="col-md-6">
      <table>
        ...
      </table>
      <ul>
        <li>Creator: Dan</li>
        <li>Launched: 7th December</li>
        <li>Planet Origin: Earth</li>
        <li>Species: Human</li>
        <li>Age: 10</li>
      </ul>
    </div>
  </div>
  <footer>
    <a href="http://www.thequestkids.com">The QuestKids</a>
  </footer>
</div>
</body>
```

Don't forget

Don't panic if it's a little messy at this stage, as we still have work to do!

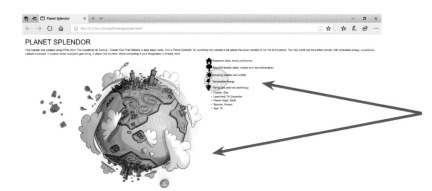

Now that we have structured our page better, our planet image should be on one side of the page, and our table and list of characters should be on the other side. It should look like this

Navigation

We now need to create a navigation menu on our website.
Most websites will have some kind of menu that allows you to navigate through the website. Because our webpage only contains one page, we will create a navigation bar that links to different pages. This menu will also adapt to cell phone and tablet sizes. We will be using Bootstrap classes to implement this.

1 Add the following lines of code underneath the page heading:

```html
<h1>PLANET SPLENDOR</h1>

<div class="row">
  <div class="col-md-12">
    <nav class="navbar navbar-light">
    <div class="container-fluid">
    <ul class="nav navbar-nav">
    <li class="active"><a href="#">Home</a></li>
    <li><a href="http://ineasysteps.com">In Easy Steps</a></li>
    <li><a href="http://www.thequestkids.com">QuestKids</a></li>
    <li><a href="mailto:hello@thequestkids.com">Email Me</a></li>
    </ul>
    </div>
    </nav>
  </div>
</div>
```

A website navigation will usually contain internal links rather than links to external websites.

You will see that we have added 4 links to our menu – Home, In Easy Steps, QuestKids & Email Me.

```html
<li><a href="#">Home</a></li>
```

This is the home link. You will notice that a href is equal to #, which basically means there is no link there, because we are currently on the homepage. This would come in handy on a larger website, when you want to navigate to the homepage from a sub page.

```html
<li><a href="http://ineasysteps.com">In Easy Steps</a></li>
```

This is the link to the In Easy Steps homepage. So we use http://www.ineasysteps.com/ under a href, and we put the text "In Easy Steps", which is what is shown in the menu.

```html
<li><a href="http://www.thequestkids.com">QuestKids</a></li>
```

This is the link to The QuestKids website. So we use http://www.thequestkids.com/ under a href, and we put the text "QuestKids", which is what is shown in the menu.

```html
<li><a href="mailto:hello@thequestkids.com">Email Me</a></li>
```

Continued ...

... Navigation Continued

This menu item is an email link. You wouldn't usually find it in a menu, but this is a good example of how you might want to implement your own email links on your website. This piece of code would open the default mail client so you could send out an email. In this case, it would open up a mail client so you could send out an email to:
hello@thequestkids.com

2 Save the changes to your document, by clicking File > Save. Your webpage should now look like the screenshot below:

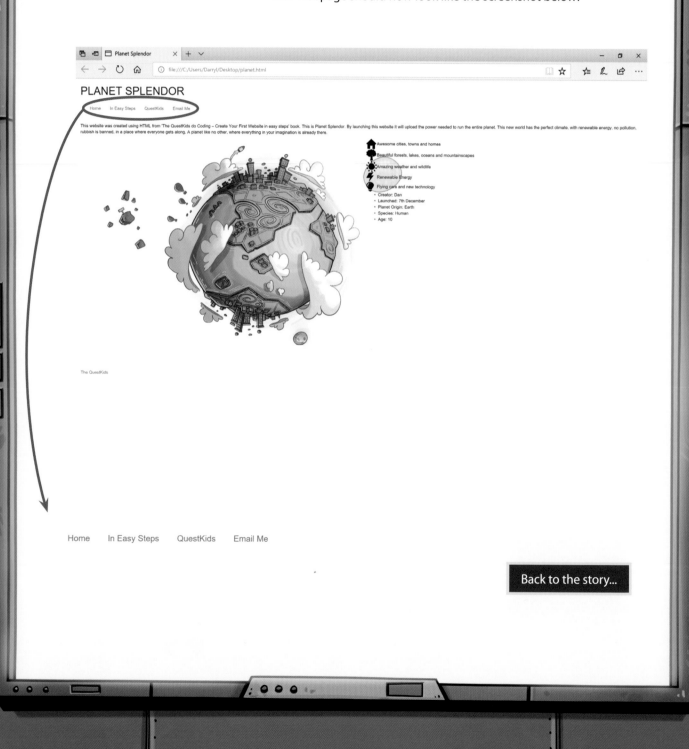

Back to the story...

Dan raced through space, hurrying towards Planet Chillico.

The spaceship entered the atmosphere and thundered towards a clearing in the snow.

"Tiff? I think he knew we were coming," said Dan as they got closer.

"Be careful Dan... he's a real cheater and I'm sure he'll have all kinds of tricks up his sleeves," said Tiff.

"Don't worry, Tiff! Right, Smuffy, prepare for a frosty welcome."

PLANET CHILLICO

The spaceship landed beside the row of flashing arcade machines. A lone figure stood next to it. Dan jumped down off the ladder as the alien leader stepped towards him.

"Dan Devices, I suspect?" said the Emperor.

"We meet again, Mr Caretaker... or should I say Emperor Ibebot! Sorry, I didn't bring your cap back," replied Dan jokingly.

"I've been expecting you. I believe you've met some of my friends?" said the Emperor.

"How do you know that?" asked Dan.

"I know everything!" he replied.

"Well, I know you have changed your spacesuit since we last met," smiled Dan.

"No thanks to your pet beast!" snapped Ibebot.

Suddenly, a ball of fur jumped out of the ship and leapt into Dan's arms. Ibebot jumped backward and almost keeled over.

"I see you remember Smuffy?" asked Dan. Ibebot regained his balance and stood well back from the dog. "So, if you really do know everything, you'll know why we're here?"

"A holiday?" replied the Emperor.

"The code you borrowed from the Space Center," said Dan, "erm... Smuffy wants it back!"

"Hmm, well I understand you have most of it. Shall we play for the rest?" asked Ibebot. "If you win, you get the last precious piece. If you lose, well, what's yours is mine."

Dan didn't hesitate to answer. "You're on, Ibebot!"

Ibebot walked towards the building. "Then follow me."

Ibebot lead them into the arcade and walked along a row of machines. "We'll play my favorite – Space Quester!" Ibebot pressed Start. Both faced the machine as battle commenced. Levels flew by, the lead going back and forth until they faced the final mission neck and neck.

"Take that, alien!" cried Dan.

"Boom! Have that, Quester!" yelled Ibebot.

Comets and rockets blasted across the screen as they fought. Dan pressed his booster button and launched a massive onslaught. A huge explosion filled the entire screen. Both players waited for the smoke to clear.

"I won!" Dan shouted.

Emperor Ibebot turned slowly towards him. "Look again," said Ibebot proudly. Dan stared at his character laid flat out as the words GAME OVER, SPACE QUESTER appeared.

"Hand it all over, loser!" said Ibebot. Dan stood in disbelief. Suddenly, Smuffy noticed a piece of paper on the floor and began to bark.

Dan gradually turned his attention to the page.

"What's this?" said Dan, as he read the title. "Cheat codes!" he exclaimed. "You cheated? You lose, Ibebot!"

"Well, m-m-maybe a little!" stuttered Ibebot. Dan looked down at his companion and mouthed a few words. Smuffy growled and suddenly launched herself at Ibebot, knocking him over. The alien froze in terror as Smuffy stood on his chest... growling!

"Code?" asked Dan.

Ibebot looked terrified. "Take this... and get that off me!" he exclaimed. Dan nodded as Smuffy slowly got off Ibebot. In a flash, Ibebot jumped up and ran off.

"Now, let's give him something to remember!" said Dan as he pulled a device off his spacebelt and threw it towards the fleeing alien. He pressed a few buttons on his wrist-tech band, and a holographic image of Smuffy suddenly appeared and raced after Ibebot. "Serves him right! Now, Smuffy, last one to the ship is a Zeeog!"

Dan's spaceship blasted into the Cosmos and made a course for Earth. "Come in Tiff! We won!"

"Woo-hoo!" she screamed. "Send me that code, pronto!"

"Will do! How we doing for time?" asked Dan. "...And any sign of your Uncle?"

"Uncle Pimlico is still stuck in the lift!" replied Tiff. "Repair men are on their way to free him though."

"Okay! We're zooming back to you now!" exclaimed Dan. "Look out for the rest of the code. I'm sending it now."

Dan scanned the page and pressed Send.

"Got it!" said Tiff a few seconds later. "Brilliant work, team! Now get back home super quick before Uncle finds out you borrowed that spaceship!"

"Copy that. Rockets to the max!!!" he yelled as they blasted towards Earth. "Home time, Smuffy!"

Finally, make your website stylish!

48

Styling

Now that we have added our elements, and structured the page, it's time to style the page. At the moment it looks a bit plain and needs some decorating!

Style Tag

Before we start adding any styles to the page, we need to create a style tag in the <head> area.

1 Add the following lines of code:

```
<!doctype html>
<HTML>
  <head>
    <meta charset="utf-8">
    <title>Planet Splendor</title>
    <link rel="stylesheet" href="https://maxcdn.bootstrapcdn.com/
    bootstrap/3.3.7/css/bootstrap.min.css">
    <style>
    </style>
  </head>
<body>

<h1>PLANET SPLENDOR</h1>

<div class="row">
  <div class="col-md-12">
    <nav class="navbar navbar-light">
    <div class="container-fluid">
    <ul class="nav navbar-nav">
    <li class="active"><a href="#">Home</a></li>
    <li><a href="http://ineasysteps.com">In Easy Steps</a></li>
    <li><a href="http://www.thequestkids.com">QuestKids</a></li>
    <li><a href="mailto:hello@thequestkids.com">Email Me</a></li>
    </ul>
    </div>
    </nav>
  </div>
</div>

...

</body>
</HTML>
```

All your styles will go in between the <style> and </style> tags.

Hot tip

You can also add your styles to an external style sheet called style.css. However, in this book we will be keeping things in the same document. You can find out more on this in the book titled **CSS3 in easy steps**. Visit **www.ineasysteps.com** for more information.

Background Image

At the moment, the page has a blank background. Let's start by adding our own background image.

1 Add the following line of code in between your style tags:

```
<style>
   body {background-image: url("http://www.thequestkids.com/space.
   jpg");}
</style>
```

2 Save the changes to your document, by clicking File > Save. Your webpage should now look like the screenshot below:

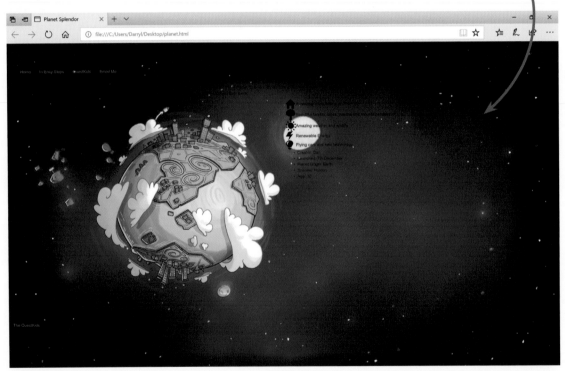

When adding your own images as backgrounds, remember to make sure the image is large enough to cover the size of the page.

Our webpage is still not tidy yet as we still have work to do.

Paragraph Text Styling

Now, we will change the color and font size of the paragraph text.

1 Add the following line of code in between your style tags:

```
<style>
  body {background-image: url("http://www.thequestkids.com/space.
  jpg");}
  p {font-size: 14px; color: white;}
</style>
```

This code will change anything within the <p> tags to the color white, and also apply a font size of 14 pixels (px).

2 Save the changes to your document, by clicking File > Save.
Your webpage should now look like the screenshot below:

When adding styles, you will need to make sure they open with a curly bracket { and close with a curly bracket }.

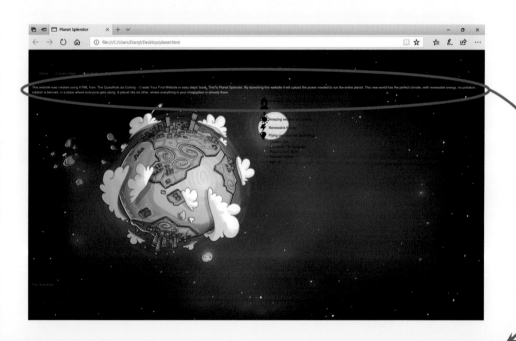

This website was created using HTML from 'The QuestKids do Coding – Create Your First Website in easy steps' book. This is Planet Splendor. By launching this website it will upload the power needed to run the entire planet. This new world has the perfect climate, with renewable energy, no pollution, rubbish is banned, in a place where everyone gets along. A planet like no other, where everything in your imagination is already there.

Link Text Styling

Next, we will change the color of the link text to black.

1 Add the following line of code in between your style tags:

```
<style>
   body {background-image: url("http://www.thequestkids.com/space.
   jpg");}
   p {font-size: 14px; color: white;}
   a {color: black;}
</style>
```

2 Save the changes to your document, by clicking File > Save.
Your webpage should now look like the screenshot below:

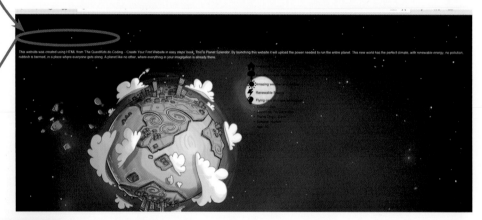

Changing Font - Google Fonts

We want our website to stand out, so we don't really want to be using the same font for each area. Let's look at applying a new font to the h1 element, which is our main heading. We will be using Google Fonts to do this. Google Fonts has a huge range of fonts for developers to use.

1 First, we need to add a reference to Google Fonts in the <head> section of our code:

```
<head>
  <title>Planet Splendor</title>
  <style>
    ...
  </style>
  <link rel="stylesheet" href="https://maxcdn.bootstrapcdn.com/
  bootstrap/3.3.7/css/bootstrap.min.css">
  <link href="https://fonts.googleapis.com/css?family=McLaren"
  rel="stylesheet">
</head>
```

Don't forget

It's still a little messy at this stage, as there is more work to do on styling!

 Continued ...

52

... Changing Font - Google Fonts Continued

2 Add the following line of code in between your <style> tags:

```
<style>
  body {background-image: url("http://www.thequestkids.com/space.
  jpg");}
  p {font-size: 14px; color: white;}
  a {color: black;}
  h1 {font-family: 'McLaren', cursive; font-size:44px;}
</style>
```

This code will change the font to McLaren, and apply a font size of 44px.

3 Finally, let's change the color to white. Add the following code:

```
<style>
  body {background-image: url("http://www.thequestkids.com/space.
  jpg");}
  p {font-size: 14px; color:white;}
  a {color:black;}
  h1 {font-family: 'McLaren', cursive; font-size:44px; color: white;}
</style>
```

4 We should also change the font of our paragraph text to McLaren, to keep the website consistent. Add the following code:

```
<style>
  body {background-image: url("http://www.thequestkids.com/space.
  jpg");}
  p {font-size: 14px; color:white; font-family: 'McLaren', cursive; }
  a {color:black;}
  h1 {font-family: 'McLaren', cursive; font-size:44px; color: white; }
</style>
```

5 Save the changes to your document, by clicking File > Save.
Your webpage should now look like the screenshot below:

Hot tip

You can find a list of fonts available from Google by going to:
https://fonts.google.com

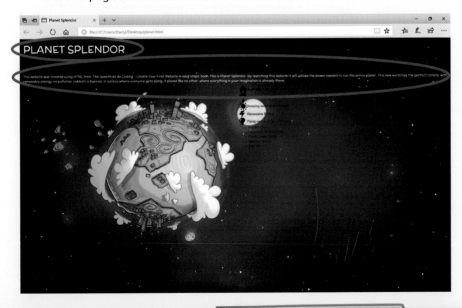

Hot tip

You can set a font weight to be normal, bold, bolder or lighter. In some cases you can also use numbers (for example: font-weight:500;). This depends on your font selection.

Font Weight

Sometimes you will want to add a bit of impact to your text. We are going to make our title bold so it stands out from the rest of the text.

1 Add the following line of code in between your style tags:

```
<style>
   body {background-image: url("http://www.thequestkids.com/space.
   jpg");}
   p {font-size: 14px; color:white; font-family: 'McLaren', cursive; }
   a {color:black;}
   h1 {font-family: 'McLaren', cursive; font-size:44px; color: white; font-
      weight: bold;}
</style>
```

2 Save the changes to your document, by clicking File > Save. Your webpage should now look like the screenshot below:

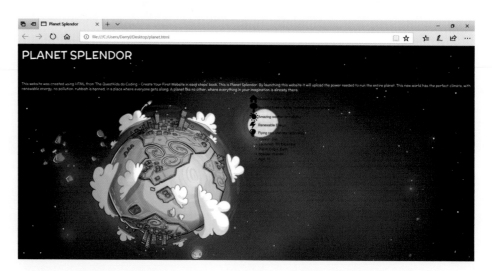

Aligning Text

Next, we will align the main header so it's centered at the top of the page.

1 Add the following line of code in between your style tags:

```
<style>
   body {background-image: url("http://www.thequestkids.com/space.
   jpg");}
   p {font-size: 14px; color:white;}
   a {color:black;}
   h1 {font-family: 'McLaren', cursive; font-size:44px; color: white; font-
      weight: bold; text-align: center;}
</style>
```

 Continued ...

... Aligning Text Continued

2 Save the changes to your document, by clicking File > Save.
Your webpage should now look like the screenshot below:

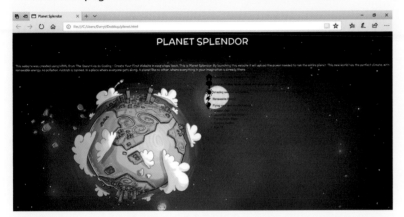

Our header centralized

You can align your text on the left, in the center or on the right-hand side.

Margins

We will now add a margin for our header. A margin will increase the space between the current element and other surrounding elements.

1 Add the following line of code in between your style tags:

```
<style>
    body {background-image: url("http://www.thequestkids.com/space.
    jpg");}
    p {font-size: 14px; color:white; font-family: 'McLaren', cursive;}
    a {color:black;}
    h1 {font-family: 'McLaren', cursive; font-size:44px; color: white; font-
    weight: bold; text-align: center; margin-top: 30px;
    margin-bottom: 30px;}
</style>
```

2 Save the changes to your document, by clicking File > Save.
Your webpage should now look like the screenshot below:

Table Styling

Earlier on in the book we created a table outlining the benefits of Planet Splendor. The next step is to style the table to make it stand out.

1 Add the following line of code in between your style tags:

```
<style>
    body {background-image: url("http://www.thequestkids.com/space.
    jpg");}
    p {font-size: 14px; color:white; font-family: 'McLaren', cursive;}
    a {color:black;}
    h1 {font-family: 'McLaren', cursive; font-size:44px; color: white; font-
    weight: bold; text-align: center; margin-top: 30px;
    margin-bottom: 30px;}
    table {margin-bottom:15px; margin-top: 15px; border: 6px solid
    black; width: 65%; margin-left:auto; margin-right:auto;}
    td {background: #d3ffff; padding: 8px 14px 14px;
    font-family: 'McLaren', cursive;  font-size: 14px;}
</style>
```

You will notice we added 2 lines here:

table {margin-bottom:15px; margin-top: 15px; border:6px solid black; width: 65%; margin-left:auto; margin-right:auto;}

This line will style the table as a whole. So in this case, we are adding a set margin of 15px at both the top and the bottom of the table. We have set the left and right margin to auto, so that it will automatically be centered inside the col-md-6 div. We are also adding a black border, and setting the width of the table to 65%.

td {background: #d3ffff; padding: 8px 14px 14px; font-family: 'McLaren', cursive; font-size: 14px;}

This line styles each table cell. So in this case, we are applying a background color of light blue to each cell. We are adding some padding, which will generate space around the content in the cells, and we are assigning a font and font size.

2 Save the changes to your document, by clicking File > Save. Your webpage should now look like the screenshot below:

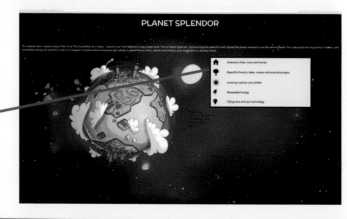

Navigation Styling

At the top of the page, we have our navigation with 4 links. Let's add a background color to make this stand out.

1 Add the following line of code in between your style tags:

```
<style>
  body {background-image: url("http://www.thequestkids.com/space.
  jpg");}
  p {font-size: 14px; color:white; font-family: 'McLaren', cursive;}
  a {color:black;}
  h1 {font-family: 'McLaren', cursive; font-size:44px; color: white; font-
  weight: bold; text-align: center; margin-top: 30px;
  margin-bottom: 30px;}
  table {margin-bottom:15px; margin-top: 15px; border:6px solid
  black; width: 65%; margin-left:auto; margin-right:auto;}
  td {background: #d3ffff; padding: 8px 14px 14px;
  font-family: 'McLaren', cursive;  font-size: 14px;}
  .navbar {background: #5ce1f0;}
</style>
```

You will notice that we have used a code for the background color rather than an actual color name. This is called a Hex code. It's a 6-digit code that represents a color.

2 Save the changes to your document, by clicking File > Save. Your webpage should now look like the screenshot below:

A good website to find the Hex code you are looking for is:
htmlcolorcodes.com

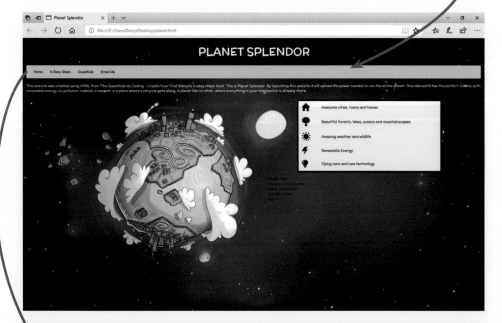

Navbar Hover Selector

Be careful not to have your hover color and text color the same, or visitors will not be able to see the text when hovering over the link.

When the user hovers the mouse over the menu links, we want the background and text color to change. This is more of a cosmetic change, but it's also so that the user recognizes what they are currently hovering over.

For this type of change we would use a:hover.

1 Add the following line of code in between your style tags:

```
<style>
  body {background-image: url("http://www.thequestkids.com/space.jpg");}
  p {font-size: 14px; color:white; font-family: 'McLaren', cursive;}
  a {color:black;}
  h1 {font-family: 'McLaren', cursive; font-size:44px; color: white; font-weight: bold; text-align: center; margin-top: 30px; margin-bottom: 30px;}
  table {margin-bottom:15px; margin-top: 15px; border:6px solid black; width: 65%; margin-left:auto; margin-right:auto;}
  td {background: #d3ffff; padding: 8px 14px 14px; font-family: 'McLaren', cursive;  font-size: 14px;}
  .navbar {background: #5ce1f0;}
  a:hover {background-color: #ffffff; color: #000;}
</style>
```

2 Save the changes to your document, by clicking File > Save. Your webpage should now look like the screenshot below:

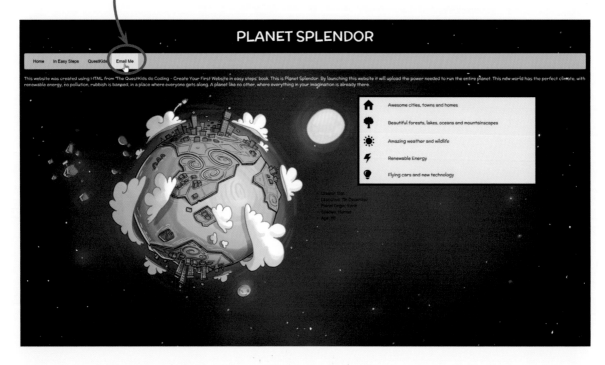

List Style

Earlier in the book we created a list underneath our table, which included your name, date etc. We will now style the list that we have printed on the page. Currently, the bullet points are circles, but we are going to change these to squares. You will also notice that the character names are currently appearing in gray, so we need to change the color to white. We will also assign the correct font and font size.

You can use various types of list styles, including square, circle and disc.

1 Add the following line of code in between your style tags:

```
<style>
    body {background-image: url("http://www.thequestkids.com/space.
    jpg");}
    p {font-size: 14px; color:white; font-family: 'McLaren', cursive;}
    a {color:black;}
    h1 {font-family: 'McLaren', cursive; font-size:44px; color: white; font-
    weight: bold; text-align: center; margin-top: 30px;
    margin-bottom: 30px;}
    table {margin-bottom:15px; margin-top: 15px; border:6px solid
    black; width: 65%; margin-left:auto; margin-right:auto;}
    td {background: #d3ffff; padding: 8px 14px 14px;
    font-family: 'McLaren', cursive;  font-size: 14px;}
    .navbar {background: #5ce1f0;}
    a:hover {background-color: #ffffff; color: #000;}
    ul {list-style-type: square; color:white; font-family: 'McLaren', cursive;
    font-size: 14px;}
</style>
```

2 Save the changes to your document, by clicking File > Save.
Your webpage should now look like the screenshot below:

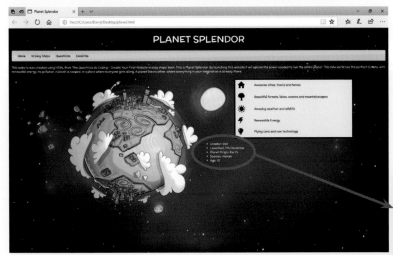

Image Sizes

You will notice that our planet image is currently too large, so we need to fix this so it displays properly; not just on desktop monitor or laptops, but also on smaller handheld devices.

❶ Add the following line of code in between your style tags:

```
<style>
    body {background-image: url("http://www.thequestkids.com/space.
    jpg");}
    p {font-size: 14px; color:white; font-family: 'McLaren', cursive;}
    a {color:black;}
    h1 {font-family: 'McLaren', cursive; font-size:44px; color: white; font-
    weight: bold; text-align: center; margin-top: 30px;
    margin-bottom: 30px;}
    table {margin-bottom:15px; margin-top: 15px; border:6px solid
    black; width: 65%; margin-left:auto; margin-right:auto;}
    td {background: #d3ffff; padding: 8px 14px 14px;
    font-family: 'McLaren', cursive;  font-size: 14px;}
    .navbar {background: #5ce1f0;}
    a:hover {background-color: #ffffff; color: #000;}
    ul {list-style-type: square; color:white; font-family: 'McLaren', cursive;
    font-size: 14px;}
    img {max-width: 100%; height: auto;}
</style>
```

❷ Save the changes to your document, by clicking File > Save.
Your webpage should now look like the screenshot below:

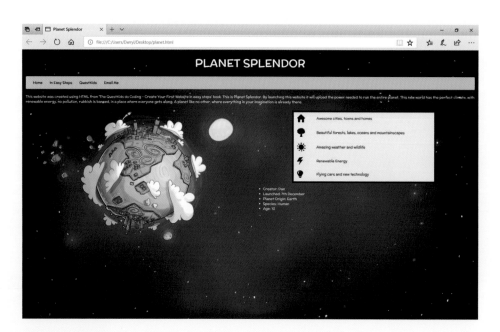

Hot tip

Sometimes you will need to experiment with image sizes to get the right variation for your design.

Image Classes

Sometimes you will want to style an image or set of images without having it affect all images on your website. Let's go back to the table of images we created earlier. In this section we are going to apply a class to each of those images, and then style that class.

1 Add the following line of code to each image in your table, just after the alt tag:

```
<table>
  <tr>
    <td><img src="http://www.thequestkids.com/iconcity.png"
    alt="Cities" class="icontable"></td>
    <td>Awesome cities, towns and homes</td>
  </tr>
  ...
</table>
```

2 Add the following lines of code to the style section:

```
<style>
  ...
  .navbar {background: #5ce1f0;}
  a:hover {background-color: #ffffff; color: #000;}
  ul {list-style-type: square; color:white; font-family: 'McLaren', cursive;
  font-size: 14px;}
  img {max-width: 100%; height: auto;}
  .icontable {margin-left: auto; margin-right: auto; display: block;}
</style>
```

3 Save the changes to your document, by clicking File > Save.
Your webpage should now look like the screenshot below:

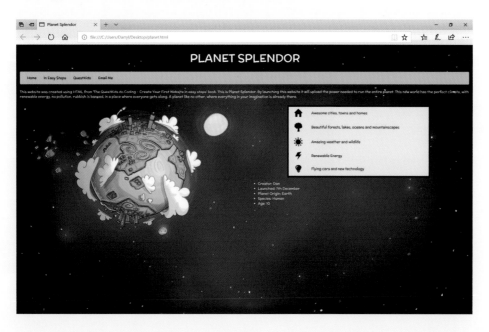

Footer Style

We will now move on to styling the footer content. We want to ensure that our footer content remains at the bottom, and that our link is displayed in the center. We also want to style our link by changing the color of the link in the footer to yellow, highlighting it in bold, and underlining it.

1 Add the following line of code in between your style tags:

```
<style>
  ...
  .navbar {background: #5ce1f0;}
  a:hover {background-color: #ffffff; color: #000;}
  ul {list-style-type: square; color:white; font-family: 'McLaren', cursive; font-size: 14px;}
  img {max-width: 100%; height: auto;}
  .icontable {margin-left: auto; margin-right: auto; display: block;}
  footer {text-align:center; clear:both;}
  footer a {color: yellow; font-weight:bold;  font-family: 'McLaren', cursive; text-decoration: underline;}
</style>
```

We have used a piece of code called clear:both; to ensure our footer link remains below the rest of the page content.

```
footer {text-align:center; clear:both;}
```

To style the link, we will need to use footer a.
This will make sure that only the style of the link in the footer is changed, and not the other links on the page.

2 Save the changes to your document, by clicking File > Save.
Your webpage should now look like the screenshot below:

Our footer centralized

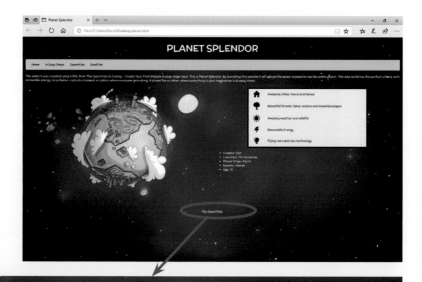

Inline Styles

You don't always have to put styles in the <style> tag at the top of the document. If you wanted a style to be applied for just one element, you might use something called an inline style. Let's have a look at applying an inline style to just our paragraph of text. We will add a margin to the bottom to provide some extra space. This style will only apply to the one paragraph.

1 Add the following line of code inside the <p> tag:

```
<!doctype html>
<HTML>
<head>
  <title>Planet Splendor</title>
  <link rel="stylesheet" href="https://maxcdn.bootstrapcdn.com/
  bootstrap/3.3.7/css/bootstrap.min.css">
  <style>
    ...
  </style>
</head>
<body>
  <div class="row">
    <div class="col-md-12">
      <p style="margin-bottom: 20px;">This website was created
      using HTML from 'The QuestKids do Coding – Create Your First
      Website in easy steps' book. This is Planet Splendor. By launching
      this website it will upload the power needed to run the entire
      planet. This new world has the perfect climate, with renewable
      energy, no pollution, rubbish is banned, in a place where
      everyone gets along. A planet like no other, where everything in
      your imagination is already there.</p>
    </div>
  </div>
</body>
</HTML>
```

2 Save the changes to your document, by clicking File > Save. Your webpage should now look like the screenshot below:

Setting up inline styles can make it harder to manage and also tough to override from the style section or external style sheets.

Make sure that you keep links on the same line to avoid any problems with the file/media location. This is especially important with the <img> and <link> tags.

Creating Page Elements

Now that we have our main styles in place, we are going to set up our own element and create a style for it. We will create a full-width box, which contains a title. Then we will write the style for it.

1 Let's start by creating the element in the code.
We will call it "bigtextarea". Add the following lines of code just before the <footer> tag:

```
<body>
...
   <div class="row">
     <div class="col-md-12">
       <div class="bigtextarea">
         <em>Congratulations!</em> Planet Splendor website has
         successfully been launched! Energy has been uploaded to this
         new planet for humans to live on.
       </div>
     </div>
   </div>
   <footer>
   ...
   </footer>
```

You will notice we have also added another tag in here, called <em>. This allows us to emphasize the piece of text that says "Congratulations!". This means we can also add a separate style for that one piece of text in the sentence.

2 Now, let's add the styles for the element in the <style> tags.

```
<style>
   ...
   .icontable {margin-left: auto; margin-right: auto; display: block;}
   footer {text-align:center; clear:both;}
   footer a {color: yellow; font-weight:bold;  font-family: 'McLaren',
   cursive; text-decoration: underline;}
   .bigtextarea {margin-top: 20px; color: white; text-align: center; font-
   size:16px; font-weight: bold; font-family: 'McLaren', cursive;}
   .bigtextarea em {color: yellow; font-size: 20px; font-style: normal;}
</style>
```

For the div called bigtextarea that we just created, we are adding a margin to the top of the area. This will separate it from the elements above. We are setting the text to white, aligning the text in the center, and changing the font and font size.

.bigtextarea em {color: yellow; font-size: 20px; font-style: normal;}

Because we added the <em> tag, we can now change the style of just the "Congratulations" text in the bigtextarea div. So we are going to make this text larger by setting the font to 20px and also the color to yellow. See this illustrated on page 65.

 Continued ...

... Creating Page Elements Continued

3 Finally, we are going to put our list of items into its own div so that it appears in a similar style to our table.

```
...
<div class="listitems">
<ul>
    <li>Creator: Dan</li>
    <li>Launched: 7th December</li>
    <li>Planet Origin: Earth</li>
    <li>Species: Human</li>
    <li>Age: 10</li>
</ul>
</div>
...
```

4 Now, let's add the styles for the element in the <style> tags.

```
<style>
   ...

   .bigtextarea em {color: yellow; font-size: 20px; font-style: normal;}
   .listitems {border: 6px solid black; width: 65%; background: #d3ffff;
   margin-left: auto; margin-right:auto;}
   .listitems ul {font-size:14px; color:black; margin-bottom: 15px;
   margin-top: 15px;}
</style>
```

.listitems {border: 6px solid black; width: 65%; background: #d3ffff; margin-left: auto; margin-right:auto;}

You will notice we are using a similar style to the table from earlier on. We are setting a black border, making the width 65% and also setting the left and right margins to auto.

.listitems ul {font-size:14px; color:black; margin-bottom: 15px; margin-top: 15px;}

Here, we are setting the list style for just the listitems div. We are setting the font size, the color and also setting the top and bottom margins to provide some spacing.

5 Save the changes to your document, by clicking File > Save.
Your final webpage should now look like this:

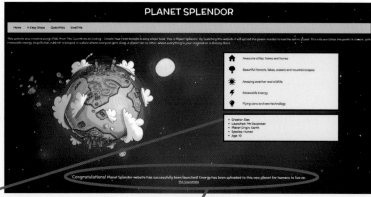

- Creator: Dan
- Launched: 7th December
- Planet Origin: Earth
- Species: Human
- Age: 10

Congratulations! Planet Splendor website has successfully been launched! Energy has been uploaded to this new planet for humans to live on.
The QuestKids

Final Source Code

Your full source code should look like this:

```
<!doctype html>
<HTML>
<head>
        <meta charset="utf-8">
        <title>Planet Splendor</title>
        <link rel="stylesheet" href="https://maxcdn.bootstrapcdn.com/bootstrap/3.3.7/css/bootstrap.min.
        css">
        <link href="https://fonts.googleapis.com/css?family=McLaren" rel="stylesheet">
        <style>
                body {background-image: url("http://www.thequestkids.com/space.jpg");}
                p {font-size: 14px; color: white; font-family: 'McLaren', cursive;}
                a {color: black;}
                h1 {font-family: 'McLaren', cursive; font-size:44px; color: white; font-weight: bold; text-align:
                center; margin-top: 30px; margin-bottom: 30px;}
                table {margin-bottom:15px; margin-top: 15px; border: 6px solid black; width: 65%;
                margin-left:auto; margin-right:auto;}
                td {background: #d3ffff; padding: 8px 14px 14px;
                font-family: 'McLaren', cursive;  font-size: 14px;}
                .navbar {background: #5ce1f0;}
                a:hover {background-color: #ffffff; color:#000;}
                ul {list-style-type: square; color:white; font-family: 'McLaren', cursive; font-size: 14px;}
                img {max-width: 100%; height: auto;}
                .icontable {margin-left: auto; margin-right: auto; display: block;}
                footer {text-align:center; clear:both;}
                footer a {color: yellow; font-weight:bold; font-family: 'McLaren', cursive; text-decoration:
                underline;}
                .bigtextarea {margin-top: 20px; color: white; text-align: center; font-size:16px; font-weight:
                bold; font-family: 'McLaren', cursive;}
                .bigtextarea em {color: yellow; font-size: 20px; font-style: normal;}
                .listitems {border: 6px solid black; width: 65%; background: #d3ffff; margin-left: auto;
                margin-right:auto;}
                .listitems ul {font-size:14px; color:black; margin-bottom: 15px; margin-top: 15px;}
        </style>
</head>
<body>
    <div class="container-fluid">

        <h1>PLANET SPLENDOR</h1>

        <div class="row">
                <div class="col-md-12">
                <nav class="navbar navbar-light">
                <div class="container-fluid">
                <ul class="nav navbar-nav">
                <li class="active"><a href="#">Home</a></li>
```

 Continued ...

... Final Source Code Continued

```html
				<li><a href="http://ineasysteps.com">In Easy Steps</a></li>
				<li><a href="http://www.thequestkids.com">QuestKids</a></li>
				<li><a href="mailto:hello@thequestkids.com">Email Me</a></li>
				</ul>
				</div>
				</nav>
			</div>
		</div>

		<div class="row">
			<div class="col-md-12">
			<p style="margin-bottom: 20px;">This website was created using HTML from 'The QuestKids
			do Coding – Create Your First Website in easy steps' book. This is Planet Splendor. By
			launching this website it will upload the power needed to run the entire planet. This new
			world has the perfect climate, with renewable energy, no pollution, rubbish is banned, in
			a place where everyone gets along. A planet like no other, where everything in your
			imagination is already there.</p>
			</div>
		</div>

		<div class="row">
			<div class="col-md-6">
				<img src="http://www.thequestkids.com/planetsplendor.png" alt="Planet">
			</div>

			<div class="col-md-6">
				<table>
					<tr>
						<td><img src="http://www.thequestkids.com/iconcity.png"
						alt="Cities" class="icontable"></td>
						<td>Awesome cities, towns and homes</td>
					</tr>
					<tr>
						<td><img src="http://www.thequestkids.com/iconforest.png"
						alt="Forests" class="icontable"></td>
						<td>Beautiful forests, lakes, oceans and mountainscapes</td>
					</tr>
					<tr>
						<td><img src="http://www.thequestkids.com/iconweather.png"
						alt="Weather" class="icontable"></td>
						<td>Amazing weather and wildlife</td>
					</tr>
					<tr>
						<td><img src="http://www.thequestkids.com/iconenergy.png"
						alt="Energy" class="icontable"></td>
						<td>Renewable Energy</td>
					</tr>
```

Continued ...

... Final Source Code Continued

```html
        <tr>
                <td><img src="http://www.thequestkids.com/icontech.png"
                alt="Technology" class="icontable"></td>
                <td>Flying cars and new technology</td>
        </tr>
</table>


<div class="listitems">
<ul>
        <li>Creator: Dan</li>
        <li>Launched: 7th December</li>
        <li>Planet Origin: Earth</li>
        <li>Species: Human</li>
        <li>Age: 10</li>
</ul>
</div>
        </div>
</div>


<div class="row">
        <div class="col-md-12">
                <div class="bigtextarea">
                        <em>Congratulations!</em> Planet Splendor website has successfully
                        been launched! Energy has been uploaded to this new planet for humans to
                        live on.
                </div>
        </div>
</div>

<footer>
<a href="http://www.thequestkids.com">The QuestKids</a>
</footer>
</div>
</body>
</HTML>
```

Your new website will only work on your own personal device and not available to other web users. You need an adult to sign up with a web hosting service to share your website.

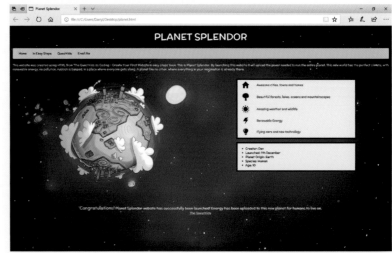

Your completed webpage should look like this.

Finishing the quest!

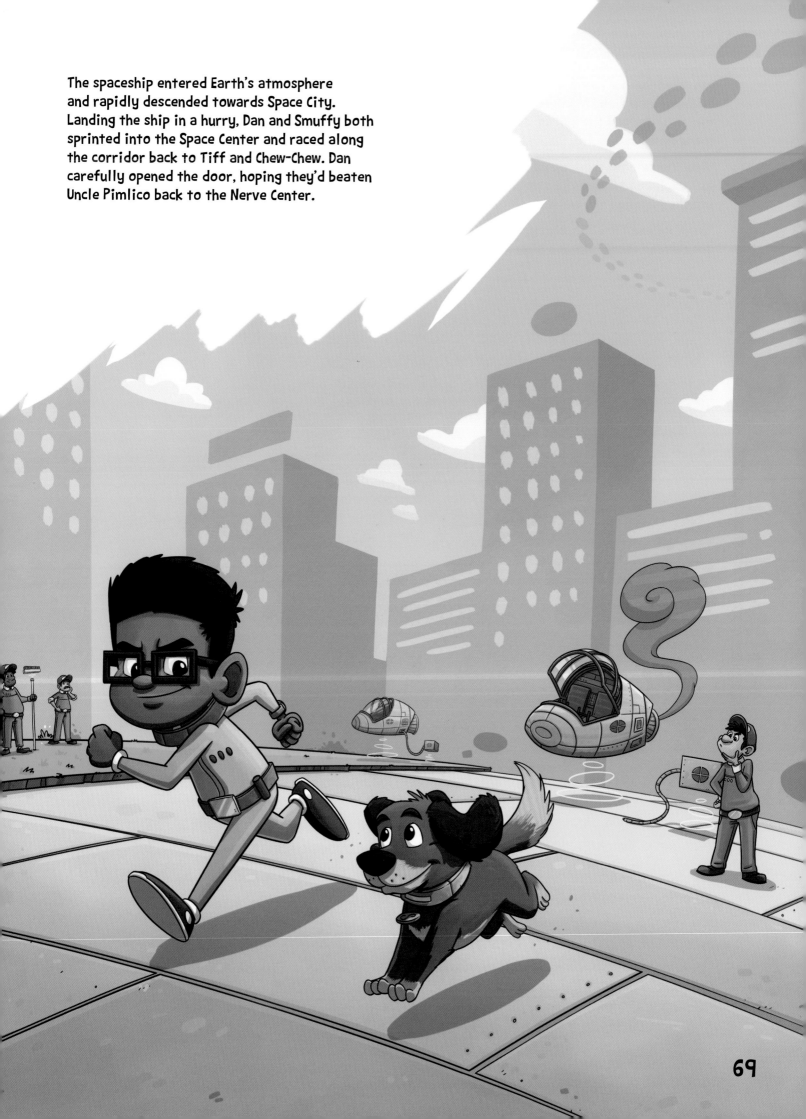

The spaceship entered Earth's atmosphere and rapidly descended towards Space City. Landing the ship in a hurry, Dan and Smuffy both sprinted into the Space Center and raced along the corridor back to Tiff and Chew-Chew. Dan carefully opened the door, hoping they'd beaten Uncle Pimlico back to the Nerve Center.

69

Dan saw that the coast was clear and burst in. Chew-Chew fired his device in a panic. Both narrowly dodged the hail of debris that flew towards them.

"Hey! There's me thinking you'd be glad to see us!" exclaimed Dan, as he stared at the debris smashed against the walls.

"Dan!" yelled Tiff. "Oh, sorry, err... Chew-Chew got carried away."

Tiff turned back to the screens. "Look! It's launched!" she screamed. "The website! It's live!"

Dan stared up at the screens and saw the website working perfectly. "Wow!" he exclaimed.

"It's amazing. We did it!" said Dan as he celebrated and high-fived the rest of the team.

Dan turned to Tiff. "Where's Unc..." Dan paused as the door suddenly flew open.

Uncle Pimlico raced in. "Hi kids. I trust you've been behaving?"

"Sure! We erm... never even left the room!" Dan winked at Tiff.

"I would have been here sooner but I got stuck in the lift... and after all that, my boss wasn't even there!" explained Uncle Pimlico.

Tiff stared at Dan and placed her finger against her lips and whispered, "Shhh!!"

"Ah! My magnificent website," said Uncle Pimlico as he stared upwards. "Sorry I missed its launch."

Dan and Tiff slumped into the nearest chairs, knowing they'd secretly saved the day.

"Uncle! Can we go home? We're exhausted!" pleaded Tiff.

"Nonsense!" he replied. "I promised you a tour."

Dan and Tiff stood up slowly and looked at each other. Tiff crouched down whilst Dan grabbed Uncle Pimlico's attention. She carefully undid Chew-Chew's ball and whispered to him. He began to squeak wildly. Suddenly, everyone stood back as he leapt towards Uncle Pimlico and bared his teeth.

"Arrrrgh! Not again!" shouted Uncle Pimlico as he flew out of the door, chased by Chew-Chew.

Tiff turned to Dan, smiled, and shouted:

"Top work, QuestKids!"